THE AUTOHOAXER HANDBOOK

Living In Truth at a Time Of Universal Deceit

By Tim Ozman
Copyright 2018

INTRODUCTION:

T his is a much-needed guide to deconstructing the real fake news the fake news doesn't want us to know about. Autohoaxing must become a standard practice. It is where the truth movement must go if it is to be be more than nominally concerned with truth.

Those who still toe the line for big media and it's astroturf counterparts are post-truth. Truth is not a destination we reach. The search is a process of constant discernment, or "living in truth."

Pseudo-science and pseudo-news create the mediated version of reality where the mediators write the rules, for they become our rulers when we accept their interpretations.

Right now, our reality is faked on CGI, scripted in news events disguised as reality, and distorted by corrupted science.

The concept of the Autohoaxing needs to go mainstream. Those of us who unapologetically take the facts as we discern them and follow where they lead without fear need to recognize what we are:

We are the new vanguard of the "truth movement",
reformers in an age of misinformation. This book is
meant to lay out the facts and makes the case that we
have to depose the new secular priesthood and the
world spanning scientocracy, or submit to it.

Whether fake trumps real is up to those of us with the eyes to see
and the conviction to challenge established falsehoods.

Tim OZman

Contents

WHY AUTOHOAX?

"In times of universal deceit, telling the truth is a revolutionary act"--George Orwell

Originally the term "Autohoaxer" was a pejorative used to describe independent researchers who assumed, based on observable patterns, that this or that latest shooting or terror attack was probably staged. The term was used derisively by those who accepted most mews stories at face value.

The autohoaxer took media criticism to a new level. Radical skepticism became the new standard. Despite the alarming number of shootings and terrorist

attacks with the same hallmarks of fakery, I continued to give the mainstream media the benefit of the doubt. It was true until proven false. But as it happened, I noticed that every single time I took the time to investigate, I found reasonable doubt as to the veracity of the media's claims.

I noticed that the notorious autohoaxers were right one hundred percent of the time. They were just the ones who took the time to look closely. Then it hit me. "Fake news" isn't merely news with an ideological bias; it's fabricated or pseudo-news events presented as real. It's

a new kind of propaganda : high-tech agitprop used to
terrify a population in peacetime into accepting the
protection of a police state while gaining approval for
the "necessity" of war to prevent terror, climate chaos,
school shootings, space junk Armageddon, or any
number of possible tragedies.

The government uses media to influence the masses with dra-
matic events intended to agitate and terrorize us. The media, is
therefore, the terrorist wing of government.

Autohoaxing is not only expedient but it is critical to
the survival of the freedom of speech itself. A secular
moral policing has fomented a new era of thought-policing, re-
vealing that for many, political correctness is more important
than a strict adherence to facts.

The Autobelievers, those who blindly accept what they
are told by the mainstream media, are a new form of
fundamentalist.

Just as religious fundamentalism becomes volatile and
dangerous to the extent that it tends towards extremism, so too
does blind acceptance of government
propaganda make the true believers dangerous and
extreme.

These hoaxed events are used to advance gun control,
suppress the first amendment, and attack independent
journalism and reporting. They justify hyper-realistic
school shooting drills designed to terrorize the children and rad-
icalize them against individual liberty.

There is no sense in expecting the media to report facts
during tragic events when the rest of what they do is
biased, partisan, corrupt, and unreliable. Don't be cowed by body

counts or bad crisis-actors.

Call it like you perceive it. If you're not autohoaxing, you're not paying attention.

THE G.A.M.E. PROGRAM

The G.A.M.E. is the interlocking and overlapping relationship between government, news media, entertainment, and cultural influences, and the worldview it creates and sustains.

This worldview is a de facto religion. It is the state religion, despite what you previously may have believed about the separation of church and state functions.

G = Government.
A = Academia.
M = Media.
E = Entertainment.

Until one can appreciate it in its entirety, one will always be in it. Surviving it requires a specific methodology and a steadfast refusal to accept authority in place of truth.

The method of seeing through and escaping the G.A.M.E. is as simple as living in the real world, which happens when truth becomes your authority. Autohoaxers are not uninformed or misguided conspiracy theorists. We are just inoculated against misinformation. We're very informed an what we're doing is a real-time deconstruction of government propaganda promulgated through corporate media every day.

This is a much needed historical revisionism, rooted in the present and preventing fake news from aggregating, unchallenged, into the accepted historical record.

We're correcting the record real-time because passively allowing the mainstream lies to pile up amounts to history. This is how they build up statistics.

This is how hysterical pundits can come out and say, "Oh, the horror! There have been 15,000 school shooting victims in six years since Sandy Hook. And it's your fault America!"

Worse, they're not really lying because, in their universe, they're citing statistics that came from sources they trust implicitly. They are in an augmented reality and people who reject the augmentations are called "deniers", which is just a new way of saying "infidel" or "heretic."

HOAX!
THE NEW BOARD
THE WHOLE FAM
CAN ENJOY!
RUN PSY-OPS!
GET RICH!
NOBODY DIES!
NOBODY CRIES!
S YOUR FAVORITE
S ACTOR! LEVEL UP!
WILL YOU FOOL THE WORLD OR WILL THE AUTOHOAXERS S

THE AUTOBELIEVER VS. AUTOHOAXER DICHOTOMY

The Autohoaxer is a person who assumes what is being presented through a medium or filter to be fake until proven real.

The Autobeliever assumes they have properly placed their trust, and that therefore they can believe what they are being shown as credible until proven otherwise.

Do you feel comfortable placing your faith in Media? Think about this: all the major MSM networks, on both sides of the political spectrum, agree that all the events we know to be false flags or psyops, are real events.

Popular pundits aren't allowed to question IF something happened. They are only permitted to opine on the thing assuming it to have happened. Opposing political factions blame the other for the latest tragic event or circumstance, meanwhile nether notice that the event was a fake, staged, pseudo-news event.

The faithful believers are not just naive, they are making the world a worse place, for the things they enable with their consent tend to be inimical to freedom and liberty.

Will you give up your freedom if the televised version of reality depicted an unsafe world that needed big
government solutions and an eventual Police State?

Too late. We already did.

Now it's time to reverse the damage done by blind adherence to the de facto State Church.

We can wake up take back our power by removing the hyper-mediated, lie-filled propaganda matrix behind; we can cease to be triggered and misguided by pseudo news and pseudoscience.

PRESUMPTION OF INNOCENCE LOST

Sir William Garrow coined the phrase "presumed
innocent until proven guilty", insisting that defendants' accusers
and their evidence be thoroughly tested in court.

With the faithful believers in the media's
misrepresentation of reality caught up in the nightly
terror stories, the presumption of innocence is not even a consid-
eration. The press, not a court of law, determine who the guilty
parties are, and what their motive is, and what reparations are
due to the victims.

The lynch mob mindset sees due process as an
obstacle and the presumption of innocence is a failsafe
against lynch-mob justice.

Anyone who followed along with the Parkland Shooting Hoax
would have observed the deliberate obfuscation of this principle
in the words and actions of the Media as well as the so called survivors. The most vocal crisis
actors were all seen expressing the sentiment that "we
all knew" that Nick Cruz would shoot up a school
someday.

Delaney Tarr, who may in fact be a role played by Cassidy Stay,

suggested that ALL the students knew
that Nick had "autism" and would be a problem later.
The blonde girl who told the news reporter that Nick was with
her when the shooting happened joked that she expected he
would be involved.

This is a common feature in these mass shooting
hoaxes: The All Knowing Mob is being hindered from
fixing things by the State and its insistence on
protecting the Individual. Mob Justice effaces our Due Process
protections.

Thiis why they are reintroducing the Mob Mentality via the sen-
sational media, where the it serves as judge and
jury----and in a sick twist the Fake Survivors went onto
60 Minutes and applauded giving Nick Cruz the death
penalty.

This "off with his head" mentality shows that
behind the telegenic facade of the March For Our Lives
movement lies a power hungry fascist mindset.

QUESTIONING the media is politically incorrect. It
makes you a conspiracy theorist in their eyes. But wait a
minute here: if we don't question the media, then they
become the mob's weapon. It accuses the mob's
enemies of things, no burden of proof behind poorly
made propaganda movies presented as NEWS, and then
the mob demands action.
SO, if we respect and live by the principle of innocence
until proven guilty, then how about we respect the Autohoaxer
who says fake, until proven real?

If we don't then we give the lynch-mob chicken-little
hearsay news-media the ability to subvert liberty. The
only ones standing up for the accused are the

autohoaxers.

BURDEN OF PROOF

L ogic requires us to shrug the burden of proof when it comes to extraordinary claims. The misinformed and the informed differ on this one crucial point. Those who trust the pseudo-news don't question their trusted sources. This leap of faith, this misplaced trust, is the basis or the entire false worldview.

The hypermediated worldview contains falsehoods, inflated death tolls, exaggerated climate change, and innumerable other threats to your security. Paranoia is normalized by the chronic media terrorism, and in fact is rewarded.

The government is openly soliciting snitches, admonishing us to "say something" should we "see something" suspicious. This was rolled out after 9.11.01, and more recently rebranded to be used to spot potential school shooters. Fear of jihadist has moved to fear of mentally unstable gun owner. Same terrorist,

TELL NO LIE

"First, to do no harm." What about tell no lie? A baseline standard for journalism. It means, don't trust any journalist who doesn't have first-hand knowledge. To do otherwise is to participate in a global echochamber built upon a foundation of fake and pseudo news which forms a de facto history.

The only way out of this echo chamber is to put truth
above appeals to authority or appeals to anonymous
sources, and reform, in your own mind, what it means to perceive
reality first and and as close to it as you can,
versus through the filters and sensors put there to
maintain keep you in.

We should only trust real journalists and real reports;
verifiable sources that are held accountable for errors. If an anonymous source is wrong, there is not an
individual to hold to account. There is no one to remove.

If you remove the ones who are not accountable, and
therefore not correctable, you end up with better
sources.

I would propose a new standard of journalistic integrity

based on that principle of forwarding no lie or unfounded claim. "Tell no lie" means recognizing that reporting off someone else's teleprompter as a source counts as a lie if what is forwarded is false. Accountability must replace hearsay.

Viewers must treat all news media stories as falsifiable. Indefinitely. Lies should have no statute of limitation. Tradition, habit, etc are not excuses for clinging to falsehoods.

We must shift the burden of proof to the reporters. We can't just auto-believe in every atrocity or threat they present and expect not to be taken advantage of. The media will play upon your emotions, specifically fear and guilt.

Question their claims, even when they throw body counts in your face.

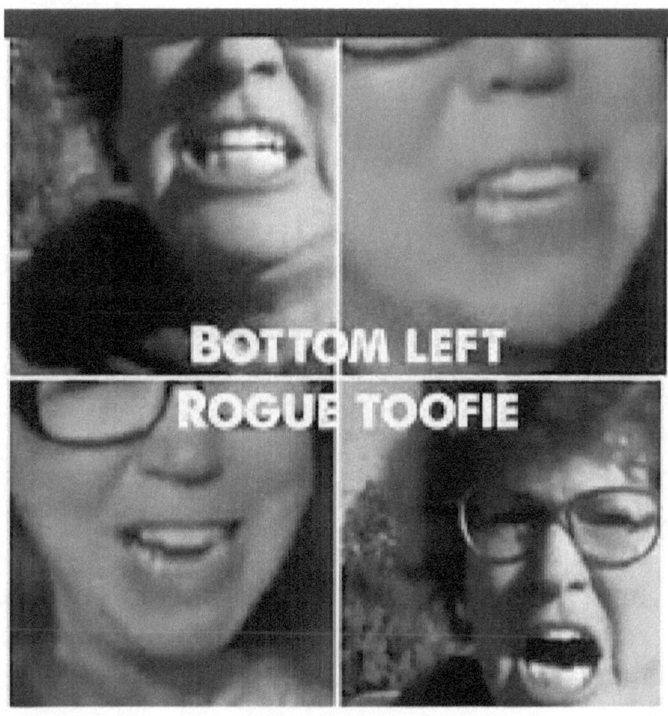
BOTTOM LEFT
ROGUE TOOFIE

ARE YOU MISINFORMED, UNIFORMED, OR INFORMED?

MSM Fundamentalism vs. Living In Truth
In the mediated reality, you are misinformed. But to the extent you are conformed to the misinformation, you are well-adjusted and experiencing cognitive dissonance.

If you are uninformed, you're a passive vessel for the misinformed, who largely shape the world you exist within. If the masses of misinformed fear that the sky is falling, you'll wind up paying taxes to mitigate their fear.

Non-participation has its price.

The default position is the dominant one expressed by the will of the majority of the misled. The uninformed are in a weak place. Ignorance doesn't shield one from the big catastrophes and leaves one vulnerable to psychological operations out of a lack of knowing the difference between real and fake news.
For that, you have to be informed. The informed recognize misinformation and know not to conform to it.

What do we do with this information?

All it takes for the misinformers to succeed is the silence of those informed enough to see through their pseudo-reality construct. The reasonable thing to do is to call out the fake and stand with real.

PSEUDO-NEWS AND PSEUDO-SCIENCE

"Truth sounds like hate to those who hate truth "
Proverbs 9:7-8

If a scientifically held belief lacks falsifiability, that is, if its closed to facts cannot be used to demonstrate it might be wrong, if new facts aren't permitted, then it's not really scientifically held.

If it's counter to new information then its counter-science. But what about journalism? Journalism isn't specifically a science but is based observing and recording of pertinent facts, and publishing the research. What does it mean when news reports are considered unchallengable?

When a scientist is wrong, the inaccurate presumptions of logical errors must be removed for the work to
continue with the integrity required of science.

But what happens when a journalist is wrong? In an honest world there would be retractions, story corrections, and amendments to be made.

In today's world, the lies of our reality mediators are not only immune to revision, but are hostile to challenge. To question the reality of a new story is now the moral equivalent to a hate crime.

WORLDVIEW WARFARE AND ROCKET SCIENCE
Your religion is your worldview. The mainstream
worldview came from Nazi rocket scientists who
created a new paradigm in the minds of the masses.

24

WHOSE-STORY IS HISTORY?

History is, by necessity, selective and curated by those that have the power to do so; the conquerors.

When we think about history, we have to consider the worldview shaping role history has, and how history itself is, and always will be, heavily contested for a myriad of reasons. Not believing one historical account is called denialism or hate.

The only logical way to proceed is to recognize the fallacy of making arguments from history, specifically recent history which is authored by mainstream media.

NOW is ground zero. NOW is where we stake our claim in reality, not on some imagined or unverifiable past. We have to abandon myths and move onto solid, epistemological ground.

We must also proceed in full knowledge that so long as the present is controlled, so too will the future be controlled. If we don't seize the NOW, the future will not belong to us, but to the technocrats who are designing a brave new world for the truly deceived.

THE MAINSTREAM MEDIATED REALITY

A nd everything that flows from it constitutes the State Church. It is a worldview framed by fake news and fake science. This worldview is a complete religion unto itself. Reporters are Worldview Reinforcers and teleprompted scripture reading and MSM Doomsayers.

It is important to realize that you are under no obligation to believe what you are told. You have the right to disbelieve, to be a non-believer. Until you refuse to believe, you cannot be a knower. When we self-mediate and seize the means of perception, faith in the fake gives way to knowledge of the real.

.

MINISTRY OF UNTRUTH

The thought policing is done by one another. Community Guidelines and user Terms of Service leave us at the mercy of anyone who decides to find a reason to flag our content.

Across all social media platforms, voices are being suppressed not by government, but by citizens radicalized by government.

Social justice warriors, those perpetually outraged and triggered moral busybodies seeking to save the world, are given the upperhand in their struggle to censor opposing viewpoints and offensive opinions. For them, calling out the sinner is a form of salvation by good works, and totally explains the phenomenon of virtue signaling behaviors and action.

Citizen-Censors have been activated by the likes of Apple CEO, Tim Cook and other giants in social media, precisely because this is an area where the public has a foothold on the means of perception.

In the MSM's desperate fight for its survival in the face of rapid disintegration and fragmentation, it has ceased defending its claims in favor of attacking non-believers. Non-believers in "climate change" are called "denialists" whose refusal to believe is considered a greater sin than climate change itself.

Tim OZman

We have to defend truth despite being called denialists.
Those who capitulate to big lies are enabling the system
of lies. Don't be a fake enabler.

Fear of offending the mob is cowardice. The mob itself
is a product of cowardice; of individuals merging
into the security of the group.

There's no reason to fear fake when you wield the truth.
As we proceed with the work of Reformation, we cannot allow sacred cows nor tradition or habit to inhibit our important work.

They may call you a denier, but the truth is, those who call seeker "deniers" for disagreeing are themselves denying facts that contradict their indoctrination. A denier is in reality a truth conduit, and appreciates truth and reality, rather than hiding it out of fear, guilt or shame.

OUR SHINING DARK AGE

We are living in a dark age and it will continue until the perceivers outnumber the blind faith believers.

Believers fear blindly and hope naively;
they **fear** of wrathful Globe and they **hope** for a gilded Heaven.

We have an entrenched Priest Class which offers Salvation at a price in an age old bait and switch scheme which offers security in exchange for your freedom.

It is only hubris and ignorance that permits us to imagine we're the pinnacle of civilization. The cure for ignorance is knowledge and the cure for hubris lies in recognizing and owning that ignorance.

MEDIAEXIT:OUT OF THE DARKNESS:

The Autohoaxers are conscientious objectors to the Psywar. We tuned out and entered a new, post-mediated era, past the imposed ignorance and superstition of a dogmatic dark age brought on by a
priesthood of pseudoscience and the inescapable
worldview reinforcers in the G.A.M.E. complex.

The only solution is a total reformation. It begins within The individual. We have to construct an account of what know to be true and what we know not to be proven.

When we mix up the two, we fall into fake-ville.
Most importantly, we have to have an elevated standard
of evidence: Fake until Proven Real.

AFTERWORD

Something needs to be said. Lots of things, in fact need to be said. Proactive voices need to rise up from the multitudes living under a spell of state imposed ignorance. It's time to wake up. There's no more excuses.

The truth is self-evident if we're willing to seek it, but more than being found, it must be defended.

You are informed. What you do with that information is up to you. Will you conform that truth to fit in with the world, or will you reform the world to conform to that truth?

At a minimum, you must be a conduit for the free-flow of Information unfiltered by the G.A.M.E. Programmers and a contientious objector to it's perpetual mindwar.

THE MAINSTREAM MEDIA IS THE STATE CHURCH

INDEPENDENT MEDIA THAT OOESN'T AUTOHOAX IS CO-DEPENDENT UPON THE MSM

THE ALTERNATIVE MEDIA IS ALL ASTROTURFED, LEFT AND RIGHT.

Brendan Kelly speaks with reporters outside his home, as he shows his Route 91 tattoo, Thursday, Nov. 8, 2018, in Thousand Oaks, Calif. Kelly, a Marine who was at Borderline Bar and Grill on Wednesday night, helped people get out after a gunman opened fire at the establishment. Kelly also survived the Las Vegas Route 91 Harvest Festival shooting in 2017. (AP Photo/Ryan Pearson)